WHAT IS PEACE?

AND OTHER POEMS

Leonore Arvidson

Edited by Enid Arvidson and Dean Arvidson
with assistance from Ben Garnett

WHAT IS PEACE? AND OTHER POEMS
Leonore Arvidson (1925–2006)

IBSN: 978-0-578-78888-3

We are indebted to William Foley and Cin Salach for their indispensable work with design and editing. Architectural photo on the cover by Athena Sandrini: https://www.pexels.com/photo/yellow-and-black-pattern-2254103/

"Tomorrow's Power Today," "To An Old Man Dying," and "Now the Wheels Are Winding Down" were previously published in *Pandemonium* 1:1, Winter 1974 (published by PAN Ltd., 157C N. LaPeer Drive, Beverly Hills, CA 90211), and reprinted here with permission. "What Is Peace?" was previously published in *Poets Against the War* and reprinted here with permission (https://poetsagainstthewar.org/). "Post Waste" was previously published in *Magazine for Kids* and reprinted here with permission.

Dates poems were written (revised):
"A Name Is a Name Is A Name" 1973; "An Image of My Mother" 1967; "Ave Atque Vale!" 1974 (2002); "Best Friends" 1973; "Cold Storage 2002; "Definition" 1973; "Despair" 1967; "Effusion" 1978; "Elegy to a Dead Voice" ND; "Fruition" 1973; "Gloom" 1974; "Happy Birthday" 1974; "Instrumental Transmutation" 1973; "Just A Thought" 1979; "L.A. Today" 1980; "Late Edwardian" 1968 (1974); "Love Song" 1973; "Men at Work" 1973 (1978); "Mother's Advice" 1978; "Normie's Lesson" 1973; "Now the Wheels Are Winding Down" 1973; "Older than Death" ND; "On Leaving" 1978; "Poem in Progress" ND; "Poem to My Mother" ND; "Pome" ND; "Post Waste" 1975; "Resurgence" 1976; "Security's Child" 1973; "Sonnet" 1978; "Still Life" 1974; "Stuck" 1974; "Talking Blues" 1973; "The Answer" 1970; "The Cop-Out" ND; "The Dinosaur" 1973 (1974); "The Entertainer" 1978; "The Lonely Hearth" 1974 (1978); "The Pulse Began to Quicken" ND; "The Question" 1970; "The Seamstress" 1974; "The Unconstitution" 1976; "To An Old Man Dying" 1973; "To Harold" 2002; "To My Daughter" 1973; "To the Cow Skull on the Side of a House" 1973; "Tomorrow's Power Today" 1973; "Twice Around" 1968 (2002); "Twice Upon a Time" 1973; "UCLA Fight Song" ND; "Unfinished" 1973; "Wedding" 1978; "What Is Peace?" 1974 (2004); "When Love Was Green and Fresh" 1974; "Would Never Be Better Than Late?" 1973.

WHAT IS PEACE?

AND OTHER POEMS

Leonore Arvidson

TABLE OF CONTENTS

THREE

FOUR

FIVE

AFTERWORD

FOREWORD

Our mother, Leonore Arvidson, wrote poems about what she knew, lived, and mused on—family, politics, parenting, friends, dreams, death, and life in post-World War II Los Angeles. Until now, only four of her poems have been published.

Appearing in mostly chronological order, *What is Peace? And Other Poems* opens with "Despair" written in 1969—amidst the Vietnam War, social unrest, and environmental crisis—and closes with "What Is Peace?" written in 2004 after decades of wars, soaring CO2 emissions, and conservative economic policies intensifying inequality. During the three decades in between, Leonore's poems reflect the contexts of the times, with humor, sadness, anger, and style.

Born in Trenton, New Jersey, to immigrant parents, Leonore moved to an ethnically diverse neighborhood in East Los Angeles when she was a young teen during the Great Depression. She was Editor-in-Chief of her high school newspaper, the *Lincoln High Railsplitter*, and that led her to working as an editor at the Los Angeles *Daily News*.

The first in her family to graduate from college, she majored in Spanish at UCLA. It was there that she met her future husband, Ben Arvidson. The poem "When Love Was Green and Fresh" vibrantly narrates, in syncopated style, their courtship in the jazz bars of Los Angeles in the late 1940s—their favorite was the 575 Club on Fairfax Avenue.

"A poet is," W.H. Auden says, "before anything else, a person who is passionately in love with language." Leonore's poem "Definition" plays with this portrayal of a poet. Her fluency in English and Spanish (with touches of Yiddish), her work as an editor, and her appetite for Modernism (in architecture and art) helped cultivate her direct, honest approach to writing.

Yet one might say that although poems come through the poet, they are not from the poet—the poet is a conduit for language the meaning of which is not fixed. In other words, to quote Leonore's favorite poet, Edna St. Vincent Millay, "The poem is the thing. Is it interesting? Is it beautiful? Is it sublime? Then it was written by nobody. It exists by itself."

This volume presents the complete collected works by Leonore Arvidson. We, her children, offer these poems (with anecdotes about their contexts in the afterword) to you, the reader, to interpret and enjoy.

ONE

DESPAIR

They're going to blow up my world,
        pollute it, poison it and
        over-populate it.
And I sit and cry and cry,
And yell and scream;
        because I don't want those
        things to happen to my world.
But no one seems to hear me.
Everyone is too busy committing suicide
        to bother to hear me.
Why is it that all of the voices of reason
        seem to reach me and pass others by,
        and I am so powerless?
I nod and I agree, but what can I do?
I go home and cry and cry because I have
        two children, too.
My husband says some people have to
        be hit over the head with a 2 x 4
        in order to get their attention.
I wonder if anyone will do that before it's
        too late?

THE COP-OUT

Everywhere I look someone is
    striking a military pose.
Is this an age of militancy?
Where do I fit in?
Inside, I am soft and feathery.
Blow too hard and I
    fall over.
Oh, I know what I know.
And am willing to allow that you do, too.
So, why must I bear arms with you?
The revolution is here, but I would
    still much rather write my poetry.
I guess I am not a woman 'for all
    seasons.'
I love the springtime, and can
    tolerate the summer and fall,
But winter is much too harsh for
    my delicate stomach.
So please forgive me, my friend, if
    I stay indoors.
For certainly, you wouldn't want me
    to throw-up on you.

TWICE AROUND

Through children we recall our past,
        vicariously relive it.
Experience is one part of life,
Another is regaining lost perspectives
        by watching children.

As we grow we lose
        the intimacy of a buttercup,
        the eye-levelness of a kitten,
        the accessibility of a handful of dirt,
yet rediscover them through children.

Watching with anxious restraint
        we see how they choose and
        with what vigor they defend their choices.
How they expose us to life's secrets!

What they learn from us is revealed knowledge.
What we learn from them is ultimate wisdom.

AN IMAGE OF MY MOTHER

An image of my mother in me
An image of her mother in her
In the early evening preparing
the family dinner
expecting my husband
Children doing homework
or practicing piano
or outside playing
or in the kitchen chatting
Handling the different foods
cooking smells arise
Not sure if I'm me or a little girl
watching her mother cook

Such timelessness in a temporal world
Will my daughter sense this
someday too?

LATE EDWARDIAN

The houses of my past
haunt the confines of my mind.
Shadowy doorways, curtained windows
murky rooms restructure in my dreams.

I wander down empty hallways
lined with profusions of doors.
Turning a knob I enter
a long-forgotten parlor.

At sight everything finely recalled:
mohair sofa, matching chair, grand piano,
console radio, child's rocker, 'king chair'
carved and covered with delicate needlepoint.

I don't linger here because rooms
from other houses compel me to them.
Rooms whose names are anachronisms now:
summer parlor, portico, music room, library.

As I sleep these houses reform upon
my mind's haunted soils. The occupants long
have disappeared. I walk alone through
the houses of my past.

THE QUESTION

Am I what I am because
I overcame adversity
or was molded by it
  or both
  or neither?

Am I what I am because
I was deprived
or advantaged
  or both
  or neither?

Am I what I am because
I avoided my weaknesses
or cultivated my strengths
  or both
  or neither?

Am I what I am because
you are what you are,
or are we separately determined
  or both
  or neither?

Am I what I am because
you perceive me as you do
or I perceive myself as I do
  or both
  or neither?

Am I the sum of my parts
or part of a greater whole
  or both
  or neither?

What answers to my questions?
What question besides
What am I?

THE ANSWER

Orange juice, scrambled eggs,
toast and butter, and coffee.

Tuna fish, white bread,
potato chips and plum.

Hamburger steak, salad,
green peas, dinner rolls,
chocolate pudding and tea.

_____ S H I T .

TWO

LOVE SONG

My father wrote love poems to my mother,
post Victorian, it's true.
Yet in twenty-five years of loving
I've written no odes to you.

Love is not love any longer.
It's meaning has lost its appeal.
By changing our view of the language
have we changed the way we feel?

Does it matter that marriage is 'open,'
or even thought of as wrong?
It wasn't the words we agreed to
that have kept us together this long.

To ask why of love is deadly,
and accounts for its present demise.
For love is an intangible feeling
that we need not analyze

So I write you this love song to tell you
that my love is alive and warm.
It's living down deep inside me
and nourished by your charm.

TALKING BLUES

We took the big bird down to Florida
to wave good-bye to the astronauts—
three red blooded American youths
taking off for the moon.
It was a blast!

There was a two hour delay in the launching
due to "technical difficulties"—
something about a pressure valve
in the fuel system.
I didn't quite catch the details.

The delay kind of upset our sleeping schedule
'cause by the time we got to bed
it was five in the a. m.
But we figured it was worth it
to keep up the boys' morale.

When they finally got the thing off the launching pad
it looked like a thousand Fourth of July celebrations
and sounded like a hundred thunderbolts crashing at once.
If there is anything living on the moon
it sure must have known that company
was on its way.

Next door to Cape Canaveral where we saw the blast-off,
there's a place called Disney World.
They got regular made-up spectacles going there
like Fantasyland, Tomorrowland and Adventureland.
But Mr. Walter Disney never came up with an act
to beat that shot to the moon!

TO THE COW SKULL ON THE SIDE OF A HOUSE

Blanched bones, bare and dried,
once cloaked with flesh and hide
with blood and brain inside,
fair play or foul when you died?

Who found you, former head,
and brought you from your bed
to fix you on this stead
and fill me with your dread?

Alive you grazed and grew,
ignored the herding crew,
scorned the boxcar, too.
Ignominies not for you.

Sallow skull, stuffed with loam,
starkly stares this bovine dome.

FRUITION (to Meredith)

In the warm cell of her family she grew,
absorbing traits and strains around her,
inserting her own uniqueness,
testing for cracks in the protective shell.

Slowly she worked her way through the required mazes,
proving that she could,
pleasing her parents,
wondering what it had to do with her.

When she reached the end, she found a beginning.
This time the choices were hers.
And so, with her pack on her back,
One day she walked away.

BEST FRIENDS (to Grace)

Once we spoke of everything,
peanuts to presidents.
We stroked each other's pain,
helped construct a universe
that met our private needs.

Then the focus blurred and changed.
The male form emerged,
captured our separate beings,
bound us away from each other.

Now we meet from time to time.
You don't entirely approve of me,
nor I of you.
So we look the other way,
sip our coffee,
ask about the children.

UNFINISHED (to C.J.)

Why do you return to haunt me?
I never hurt you...
nor held you.
Long ago my daisy eyes adored
your cryptic smile,
though more than a valley of years
stretched between us.
That was part of a season
past and forgotten.

Last year I read that you had died.
Too bad, I thought,
another old friend gone.
Now I don't look for you in crowds
nor ask quite casually
how you are.
So why do you still pace my dreams
and stalk my mind?

If I had held you, could my heart
now let you go?

TO AN OLD MAN DYING

Take your sleeping pill, dear,
so you won't waken in the night
to think about the past
and cry again.

Your life has not been sadder than most,
it's simply over; and the night's
silver silence pierces
the heart's secret sorrow.

So swallow it, dear,
however bittersweet the taste,
and save your tears for—
when?

SECURITY'S CHILD

"Those who give up liberty for the sake of security, deserve neither liberty nor security."
————Ben Franklin————

Security's child

> always pays insurance premiums
> never misses doctors' visits
> always takes vitamin pills
> never talks to strangers
> always locks doors and windows
> never walks alone at night
> always drives within the speed limit
> never risks original ideas
> always fastens safety belts
> never loves too hard

Nothing risked
Nothing claimed

INSTRUMENTAL TRANSMUTATION

The telephone transforms
some of us
from reasonably reserved
to egregiously gregarious;
from familiar friend
to clipped conversant;
from timorous taciturnity
to violent volatility.

An insidious substance
circulates through
the telephonic system
propagating widespread
schizophrenia
in those sending the message
and perverting to depressive
paranoia
those receiving it.

TOMORROW'S POWER TODAY

Concrete sea wall
concealing havoc lurking
where migrant swallows
leave empty nests;

Hissing steam
manufacturing endless light
for brooding hen cities
unable to tell day from night;

Chain links
delusionary quarantines
against deathly rays
transforming vital cells
into defiled corpses;

Bubble dome house
whose bombarded inhabitants
rage against their captors
waiting to retaliate
for being racked and torn apart
to nourish hideous robots;

San Onofre
sterile conception
moribund birth

Listen
the sun is setting
it will be dark.

NOW THE WHEELS ARE WINDING DOWN

Now the wheels are winding down
Golden robots turn to brown;
Global villages disband
within the insulated land.

Crusted concrete cracked and bare
Crumbled dreams cemented there;
Towering junk heaps testify
to the day the wells run dry.

Fortune's wheel alone still goes
Where it stops no one knows;
Prophecy by truth belying
first the mourning, then the dying.

Past and future stand allied
Man and ape walk side by side;
Wisdom's warning falls ignored
so ends the year of our Ford.

WOULD NEVER BE BETTER THAN LATE?

This isn't my locker
I can't open it

I'm late.................I'm so late.............

Try the combination again
.......slowly.......
Turn the dial all the way around
Past Go
Past Mediterranean Place
Past the Railroads

That damn card again
Go to Jail
Go directly to Jail
Do not pass Go
Do not collect $200

Where are they holding the exam?
I could pass it
if only I could find it
I'm late.................I'm so late.............

A NAME IS A NAME IS A NAME

My mother called him Richard
though he was born Poor like Honest Abe.
He strove to merit the noble name
that Great William had so embellished.
With a Heart as strong as a Lion
he worked to Open the Door of opportunity.
No ordinary John Doe did he turn out to be,
but a formidable Richard Roe.
Today he dwells in George's City
applying the wisdom of the Almanacs
to his ayes and nays————————————
mostly nays, for he always searched harder
for things to put his nix on.
Ah, my Dear Dick, what's in a name?
Practically nothing.

DEFINITION

I'm in love

I'm in love with sound

I'm in love with the sound of words

I'm in love with the sounds of my own words

I'm a poet

NORMIE'S LESSON

Normie ate his dinner up,
each morsel he did swallow.
He knew if he devoured it all
a Hershey bar would follow.

"Good boy!" his mother said to him
and handed him the candy.
In the pocket of his shirt it went
so he could keep it handy.

"I think I'll go to play," he said,
"and later have my treat.
I'm much too full of dinner now
to want a thing to eat."

But as he played around the yard
and bounced his big red ball,
an urging sent him in the house
to answer Nature's Call.

And then the tragedy occurred!
As Normie pressed the lever
his Hershey bar fell in the bowl
and washed away forever.

The lesson Normie learned that day
will never be surpassed:
Always eat the best thing first
and save the worst for last.

TWICE UPON A TIME

Clasping my misty memories
I grope for an anchor in time:
    time the kind friend,
    time the adversary.

I've been here before,
    marched to this music,
    worn that gown,
    heard those words.

Words that describe a future
    impatiently anticipated
    that came and passed.

But those messages didn't
    provide for today:
The day my child, my first born
    walks to the podium,
    receives her diploma,
    confronts her dreams.

TO MY DAUGHTER

Little girl with velvet brown eyes
     I watched you come alive
          pop open like a spring wildflower
              and reach for the sun.

Radiant girl with warm brown hair
     I heard you cry of hunger
          laugh with pleasure
             sing to the world
               your new learned songs.

Tender girl with rose glow skin
     I held you
          when you felt the pain
             of rejection and loss.

Grown girl I step aside
     you pass me by.

THREE

WHEN LOVE WAS GREEN AND FRESH

When love was green and fresh
        and the city was ours
        every night of the week,
we ran marathons around the jazz bars
        lapping up music and beer,
downed Hollywood's pablum straight
        without a chaser,
caroused boulevards and back alleys,
        so strong were we together.
From the highest hill the city's lightening
        struck passion through our veins
and the greatest torture was saying
        good-bye.

So we took love
        institutionalized it
                in order
                        to avoid
                                the pain.

AVE ATQUE VALE! (To my Dad)

I've come to say good-bye.
You started leaving a couple of years ago.
Now it's final, doors closed behind you.
Those last anxious visits over,
when I did most of the talking,
urging your eyes to come alive and answer mine—
that barest thread snapped, too.

For a while I could visit and talk with you
and still enjoy that wry humor you never lost,
as once when you were hungry,
and I offered you a cup of coffee,
you looked at me as though I were a child again,
saying, "Is coffee something to eat?"

To me you were source, provider,
guardian, constraint.
You presented a world warm and beckoning,
and I rushed to meet it.
Now in grief I say farewell
and let you go forever.

POEM TO MY MOTHER

If I lay a poem on my mother's grave,
will she know I wrote it for her?
I don't believe in ghosts or spirits
or afterlife, so is it hopeless then?
I guess she'll never know about my poem.
But wait! My mother isn't in that grave.
Nor is she a ghost nor a spirit hovering in the air.
She is my poem, and my poem is my mother.
And I feel closer to her now than ever
I did in her life.

OLDER THAN DEATH

Sun light strikes five
and something not living
burns a cold bare flame
into my eye.

Dust of the earth,
from which I come, to which I must return
I hound you in mountain streams
and desert washes.

I stalk these wild rocks that burrow
and surface, that crumble and fuse.

GLOOM

The dank, dark drizzle drove through my flesh.

I felt the rain walk upon my bones,

each icy drop piercing to the marrow.

THE SEAMSTRESS

Interknit, possessed in common,
we live out of each other's pockets.
Then what would I do without you?
Desert our cause? Lower our flag,
too weak to carry it alone?

Or should I now build
a fortress of my own?
Sew a flag of a different color,
embroidered with a coat all mine?
Defend it, guard it just for me?

Would that then make me
mistress of my realm,
content to wear a crown
of self-sufficiency?

Or would I soon be standing guard
upon the prison of my soul?

STILL LIFE

Slanted sun rays stream through the glass and spread
bright warmth across the dark disordered desk.
Papers sprinkled with poems in process
lie yellowing in the mellow lights.
A ball point pen peacefully
rests in preparation of
new outpourings.
Silver scissors
sit extended
sparkling
in the sun's beam.
The tan toned telephone
stands tirelessly waiting to
jangle nerves into the present.
Time is tabulated by a calendar
calling out the current date, as hands
of a contemporary clock calculate the moment.
In the corner carefully and carelessly disregarded waits
a copious pile of unpaid bills and unanswered correspondence.

HAPPY BIRTHDAY

Remember when skirts were long and hair was short
        and swallowing goldfish the latest sport;
   when movies were silent and radio roared
        and cars were something the rich could afford;
   when sex was dirty and the air was clean
        and children weren't heard but only seen;
   when music was swinging and Sinatra crooned
        and teenagers screamed, fainted and swooned;
   when a man in uniform was in style
        and we started the day with Ernie Pyle;
   when houses were new and all in a row
        and families moved in and started to grow;
   when we had to be careful before the pill
        and no one could live on the G.I. Bill?

Can you remember all that if you really try?
Because if you do, you're much older than I

POST WASTE

I like to get mail, a happy sensation
like getting a present each day.
I open the box with warm expectation
to see what the creditors say.

One day the ads are from Penney's and MayCo.
The next day from Macy's and Sears.
And then comes a bill that I hurry to pay so
no thirty day notice appears.

I answer it all, for this I believe:
The one who responds will surely receive.
But mail that leaves me most puzzled and hesitant
comes addressed to occupant, owner or resident.

STUCK

i like

it here

it's nice here

it's cozy here

it's not here

i don't like

it's who

it who pushes pins

in me to tell me

i'm not supposed to like

it here

RESURGENCE

Lying limp
spatially buffered
in a neutral zone
       healing
       healing

Thought transplants
fabricating a
patchwork mind
       healing
       healing

Scar tissue
on scar tissue
sutured strength
rethreading hope
       healing
       healing

To rise again
       healing
       healed
       whole

THE DINOSAUR

The dinosaur walked down the street,
looked around and weeped and weeped.
Where was his forage, where the field?
Concrete covered, asphalt sealed.

A bluebird saw him and asked why
a great big dinosaur should cry.
"If you're lost, can't find your home,
go back along the road you've come."

"You can't go back, you stupid bird.
Everybody knows that's absurd.
The hands of the clock turn one way;
the earth revolves the same each day."

"Then stay right here; you needn't go."
"And starve to death? Thank you, no!"
"So you're lost," the bird said with pity.
"Me? Lost? Why, I built this city!"

"Well, stop your crying. Plan your move.
Indeed, your future could improve."
The monster sobbed, "Don't torment me.
I'm a dinosaur, can't you see?"

THE UNCONSTITUTION

Where is it written that our nation shall be divided
        into classes
                        upper
                              middle
                                    lower

Where is it written that our cities shall be divided
        into enclaves
                        racial
                              ethnic
                                    economic

Where is it written that our people shall be divided
        into opposing camps
                        white vs black
                              man vs woman
                                    young vs old

Where is it written that our workers shall be divided
        into ranks
                        professional
                              skilled
                                    unskilled

Where is it written that our children shall be divided
        into intelligence groups
                        smart
                              average
                                    dull

Vacuous tenets haunting our land
unconstituting what was carefully planned
live and die in the minds of our countrymen
                    EX UNO PLURA

FOUR

SONNET

Through the dense forest of the night
where sleep lurks among the giant trees
but keeps her face well screened from sight,
I wander searching for that somnolent peace
and stumble over skeletal remains.
I stoop to throw some dirt upon the bones,
then realize the gesture is in vain.
A haunting voice solemnly intones:
You cannot bury us, we are not dead.
We live in this dark unfrequented space
where those pursuing sleep will sometimes tread
and think they've found a final resting place.

But the forest thrives, it is not hallowed ground;
it's where the past survives and memories abound.

EFFUSION

Turn to the source
Locate the wellspring
Open the floodgate
Plunge into the stream

Outrace the current
Surmount the tide
Ride high the waves
Swim for the shore

Blot up the blooddrops
Dry up the teardrops
Unfold the Rorschach
Behold the self

ON LEAVING

You leave, have left, will leave me
     an action I deplore.
"Don't be sad," you said, not knowing
     I rage against a closing door.

Leave me and I am diminished.
Leave me and I am bereft.
Leave me and I am abandoned.
I can't contend with being left.

But let me do the leaving
     and you remain behind,
then parting is 'sweet sorrow'
     of an unavoidable kind.

I am the child who cannot end the party;
I am the daughter who never learns to mourn;
I am the mother who rocks an empty cradle;
I am the woman forsaken and forlorn.

THE LONELY HEARTH

In the morning the houses stand alone,
giant storage lockers,
umbilical cords plugged
into automatic cleaners
who sanitize and purify
accumulated inventories.

Now and then new deliveries.
Overstocks dispensed.
At times antiseptic contents
of one exchanged for another.

In the evening the owners return,
unlock their treasuries,
eat recalefied dinners
from discardable trays,
recreate with electronic imagery,
sleep, rise and leave again.

Still the houses stand,
echoing mechanical voices.
Their spotless hearths
empty and cold.

MEN AT WORK

We rejected the supernatural
          and created the superman
     made him master of earth's forces
               disdainful of nature's secrets
      faithful to button and switch

We banished frailty and error
              sins of the past
       and wallowing in power
   set out to improve the universe

We put up signs: Men at Work
                    Do not Disturb
                    Do not Question
We kept absolute faith

But the exiles stand within our borders
         unabsolved by our high priests
               committed and waiting

     for the mind to crack
        for the blood to ooze
             for the fatal error to escape

MOTHER'S ADVICE

Don't forget to make your bed
It's one of the rules of the house
I know it's unfulfilling and bland
I know it's not in keeping with the trend
I know it's insignificant and mean
I know you prefer the rumpled sheets
I know it drains your energy and drive
I know you're not a servant or a slave

Fulfillment lies in liking what we do
A well done job can be its own reward
If we work with diligence and care
We may find pleasure in our chore

Reflecting on life's growth
Don't overlook routine
That's tasting of the honey
Without crediting the bee

Fashions of the time
May dictate dos and don'ts
But subservient in fact
Is the follower of modes

So don't forget to make your bed
And make it well
For you, my child, must lie in it

THE ENTERTAINER

Arriving late she laughed open the door
        blew random kisses
        around the room
'Welcome to the party,' the revelers exclaimed
        'have a drink, meet the crowd'
        (but don't forget the act)
'Sorry I'm late, another party,' she said
        Yes, we know, we understand
        (but don't forget the act)
'Thirty years in show biz and still going strong'
        Congratulations and all that!
        (but don't forget the act)
She wove her way to the piano and warmed the keys
        with Friml and Lehar
        and some old show tunes
Picking her cue she turned toward the guests
        'Tonight I will do
        a little Marlene Dietrich'
With husky voice she sang of broken hearts
        fickle men, forsaken women
        and falling in and out of love
When she stopped they gushed praise and adoration
        'That's Dietrich,' she reminded
        'That's not me'
'More, more,' they begged and again she sang
        this time in German, so they missed
        the words but not the meaning
At the end they mouthed kisses and coos
        told her they loved
        her marvelous style
'That's Dietrich,' she said again
        'That's not me'
No one thought to ask her who she was

JUST A THOUGHT

The intense stage of initial choices was over.

We waited breathlessly to see if they would work.

They seemed to,

so we set out congratulating ourselves.

Then we spent our time caring for

and embellishing the physical plant

in order to prolong its life.

But in the end what can you say about a life

spent in prolonging itself?

L.A. TODAY

Silence harps in the streets of L.A.
      like a dried up waterfall.
Wheels no longer fly up and down
      the city's stairways.
Healing souls crouch beside fireplaces
      eyeing truths of their creation.
Gone the enchantment.
Gone the respect.
Human artistry reduced
      to a sign:
      "Out of Gas."

POME

Oil and gas no longer abound

They've pumped so much out of the ground.

But I don't care if no more is found

It's love that makes the world go round.

HAPPY VALENTINE'S DAY

WEDDING (to Sandra)

I

The young unvirgin bride
    dressed in spotless white
joins in the antique ritual

Ten minutes ago she was a child
    starting to unravel
the thread of life

Now she stands assured
    anchored to the moment
clear eyes focus outward

She is the only bride
    ever to have wed
on the face of the earth

There is no past
    only this moment
and tomorrow

II

Through clouded eyes
    I watch her
walk down the aisle

So young, she has lived
    her whole life
while I lived a third of mine

I founder in misted thoughts
    of all the brides I have known,
of all the brides in history

She is all of them
    this child in white
who does not see me

For I am the past and perceive
    only this moment
and yesterday

FIVE

UCLA FIGHT SONG

HERE COME THE BRUINS — GO!
WE'LL BE A SHOE-IN, SO
GIVE US A CHEER
GIVE US A HAND
THIS IS OUR YEAR
STRIKE UP THE BAND!

HERE COME THE BRUINS — BOLD
CHECK OUT OUR BLUE 'N' GOLD
CRASHING THE GATE
RUSHING THE LINE
MEETING OUR FATE
DOING JUST FINE!

FOUND OUR PLACE IN THE SUN
GOT THE FOE (S.C., THE BEARS, ETC.) ON THE RUN
NOW WE'RE NUMBER ONE
YOU BET! NO SWEAT!

HERE COME THE BRUINS — YEP!
WE'RE GETTING YOU IN STEP
FOR THE BIG SCENE
THIS IS OUR DAY
FOLLOW THAT TEAM
U C L A !!!!!!!!

ELEGY TO A DEAD VOICE

A voice in me died
It shot its icy pearls at the moon
    and withered away.

Each day I listen for a whisper, an echo, a tone
    from the dark side of my soul.
I hear only dust scraping a desert floor.

I try to soothe my parched throat
    with sweetened lozenges
hoping it will regurgitate one more poem.
All it expels is fetid breath.

Play me a symphony, a concerto,
    a prelude, a nocturne.
Dance me a dance to clear my eclipsed eyes.
Sing me a hymn to cauterize my bleeding ears.
Teach me again to rise from sullen earth when day breaks.

Let us return to the beginning
and reconstruct this process.
    "Twinkle – twinkle – little – star —
    How – I – wonder – what – you – are."

A voice in me has died.
It dropped its icy pearls on my heart
    and withered away.

THE PULSE BEGAN TO QUICKEN

April arrived the other day
and the ice began to melt in the heartland,
filling rivers past their brims
overrunning lowland
flooding fields and towns
drowning helpless beasts and brave rescuers
washing away seeds of life
leveling the works of man
building mountains from grains of sand
muddying rain cleansed.

COLD STORAGE

Last night you put all of your sandpaper
in the refrigerator along with other tools
and equipment. When I went to get
the milk I couldn't find it because
you had pushed it so far back.

I was expecting my sister and her husband
to arrive for a visit and I wanted to serve
some coffee and refreshments.
But I couldn't find the milk.

Then I noticed that you set up a tray
with beverages and cookies.
You used all the silver service your
parents gave us over the years
which I so thoroughly dislike.

I started to transfer things on the tray
into pottery or glass or stainless containers.
Then I heard the car. Oh, my god, I said.
Will one of you kids put the cat out?
You know how afraid of felines your aunt is.

My son put the cat out, but since the side door
was open she came right back in.
Help, I yelled. And my daughter
picked up the cat, took her out to the
garage and locked her in the car.

It turned out not to be my sister
and her husband but a group of our friends.

One of them greeted me but
mispronounced my name
and I let him have it!
You've known me for twenty years
and you can't pronounce my name?
It's three syllables just like yours!

Then your elderly father who was
sitting there looking at me said:
How can you be so rude to your friends?
And why aren't you using the beautiful
silver we've given you over the years?

Well, there's always a way out of a nightmare.
                    I went around the kitchen, smashing
        everything on the shelves, pulling
                            the contents from the refrigerator
            onto the floor, dumping the tray
                            of refreshments into the garbage,
        and I woke up.

POEM IN PROGRESS

Steeped in Father Freud,
Seasoned with the Disciples,
Spiced, sauced and pickled with the
Latter Day Saints
Sensitized and analyzed
Freda ascends the tallest building in the world
in search of self-identity and realization.
She finds glass and steel, steel and glass
looking out upon infinity—among other things.

So she rides the automated elevator down—
down to the fun house for a few laughs
and finds her reflection in the mirrors,
short / tall / thin / fat
a grotesquerie of her physiognomy.
She screams and runs out.

Norman discovers Freda
writhing in the mud, wracked with pain,
and asks her to be his wife,
or mother, or sister, or aunt, or girlfriend.
"Foiled!" cries Freda.
"I do not exist in terms of you.
I have my own label—Freda—
authorized and legalized
by the state in which I was born."
Norman has no choice but to leave.

Freda sets sail on an ancient river
that leads to myths of the past.
The river is calm, the boat rocks gently.
Freda almost falls asleep.
Suddenly the boat springs a leak
and capsizes leaving her churning
in the inky waters until
she floats ashore.

She considers giving up her search
but doesn't know how.
Remembrances of peer indoctrination
press upon her forcing her
to look for answers to what seem impossible questions.
Exhausted, Freda falls asleep and dreams.

TO HAROLD

Winter in my heart

Winter on the calendar

December 21

You died today

WHAT IS PEACE?

What is peace?
            Where is it found?
The centuries have searched
      and unearthed words and words
like empty coffins riddled with maggots,

      red dripping
            rhetoric from
drained documents telling
      war's end, smashed legalisms
spattering putrefied inequities;

      and still war,
            violent war
mightier than all the
      words of all the voices
roaring, tumbles onward, drowns innocence,

      leaving us
            the peace of death.

AFTERWORD

Poetry means making a connection —June Jordan

These anecdotes about many of the poems in this book aspire to illuminate the connections that are the heart of Leonore's poems.

"Ave Atque Vale!" and "To An Old Man Dying" and were written for Leonore's father, Michael Charnofsky, who settled in Los Angeles as an adult after migrating to Ellis Island from the Ukraine as a teenager, who recounted stories from his childhood in the book *Jewish Life in the Ukraine* (1965 Exposition Press), and who spent the last years of his life with Alzheimer's disease.

"Best Friends" was written for Leonore's best friend in college, Grace (Tracey) Vanderpool, who introduced Leonore to the man who became her husband and life partner, Ben.

"Cold Storage" included a handwritten note from Charles Muscatine, Chaucerian scholar, dated December 16, 2002, that said: "Dear Leonore: I love 'Cold Storage' altogether—witty, satirical, and technically I think just about perfect."

"Fruition" was written for the daughter of one of Leonore's life-long friends, Meredith Wambaugh.

"Love Song" and "When Love Was Green and Fresh" were written for Leonore's husband and love of her life, Ben, who died prematurely at the age of 54.

"Normie's Lesson" was written for one of Ben's lifelong friends, Norman Rudolf.

"Poem to My Mother" was written for Leonore's mother, Sophie.

"Post Waste" was written for and originally published in *Magazine For Kids*, a handwritten publication produced by Leonore's then-ten-year-old nephew Eric Charnofsky. In her cover letter to ten-year-old Eric that accompanied the poem, Leonore said: "I very much enjoyed receiving the latest issue of your magazine in the mail yesterday. I think your magazine is one of the best I've ever read, and I should like to express my appreciation. Receiving *Magazine For Kids* in the mail inspired me to write this poem which I should like to have you consider for publication in some future issue if you feel it measures up to the quality of the rest of your material."

"Talking Blues" was written about Ben and Leonore's 1972 trip to Florida to observe the launching of Apollo 17.

"The Entertainer" was written about Leonore's friend and neighbor, the actress Virginia Christine.

"To Harold" was written for Leonore's brother, Hal Charnofsky, sociologist and one of the Charnofsky twins who played baseball for the University of Southern California and New York Yankees.

"Twice Upon a Time" and "To My Daughter" were written for Leonore's daughter, Enid, upon graduating from high school and coming of age.

"U C L A Fight Song" was written for Leonore's alma mater where she met her husband, Ben.

"Unfinished" was written for a fellow editor with whom Leonore worked at the *Daily News*.

"Wedding" was written for the daughter of one of Leonore's life-long neighborhood friends, Sandra Kinsler.